# The Hour of the Poem Poem

**Also by New Academia Publishing**

*THE WHITE SPIDER IN MY HAND: Poems,* by Sonja James

*THE ALTAR OF INNOCENCE: Poems,* by Ann Bracken

*THE MAN WHO GOT AWAY: Poems,* by Grace Cavalieri

*IN BLACK BEAR COUNTRY,* by Maureen Waters

*ALWAYS THE TRAINS: Poems,* by Judy Neri

Read an excerpt at **www.newacademia.com**

# The Hour of the Poem Poem

## Poems on Writing

### David Bristol

Washington, DC

Copyright © 2015 by David Bristol

New Academia Publishing 2015

All rights reserved. No part of this book may be reproduced or transmitted in any form or by any means, electronic or mechanical, including photocopying, recording, or by any information storage and retrieval system.

Printed in the United States of America

Library of Congress Control Number: 2015942377
ISBN 978-0-9864353-8-6 paperback (alk. paper)

 An imprint of New Academia Publishing

New Academia Publishing
PO Box 27420, Washington, DC 20038-7420
info@newacademia.com - www.newacademia.com

For Patty

# Contents

| | |
|---|---|
| Another poem that will never forgive me | 2 |
| "I knew the man who wrote this poem" | 4 |
| It is the hour of poem poem | 6 |
| I write for an audience of one | 8 |
| The poem is a relentless nag | 10 |
| Not in the moment, not yesterday, not tomorrow | 12 |
| I cannot get out of the way | 14 |
| This is a found poem | 16 |
| It is laughing as I sit in the dark | 18 |
| It is shouting at me | 20 |
| For I do not want to take this with me | 22 |
| Oh shit | 24 |
| First obsession then art | 26 |
| I am writing this without me | 28 |
| An elegy for what never was | 30 |
| The air is quiet | 32 |
| This crusade is becoming a bore | 34 |
| It is a poor imitation | 36 |
| Dirty with words I am unclean | 38 |
| The page is a wall on which nothing sticks | 40 |
| Between plodding and mania | 42 |
| I am here without flowers | 44 |
| Little control of what gets onto the page | 46 |
| Without an image to live up to | 48 |

| | |
|---|---|
| The grand finale has a smile and a tear | 50 |
| Buried alive is my current state | 52 |
| I read a poem and then another | 54 |
| There is snow on the ground | 56 |
| I believe in the system | 58 |
| Up the air I leave you | 60 |
| | |
| About the Author | 63 |

Another poem that will never forgive me.
It is the way it is.
I give it words
And take its song.

Sorrow and hope,
We are here together
Pushing a modest tune,
A shout and whisper.

Sin against these words
With absence and desire.
Over the hill and wanting
More and more and more.

I sit before you,
Hands open, heart on guard,
Bringing you to this party
As your truculent date.

You have known this all along.
The song may sweeten,
But it is not free.
I seek to bargain.

As one not quite happy with your offering,
You know I make ridiculous claims.
All is not new,
Some of it is blue.

So you spurn me
For wanting too much
From only a poem
Written on a quiet day.

"I knew the man who wrote this poem."
We have drifted apart.
He rarely says hello.
He has a garden gnome.

I suppose I am the one at fault.
I have filled every gap with silence.
I never pick up the phone.
What can I say?

It is tomorrow today
And I will make a call
To inquire about his health.
A first gesture.

The burden of reconciliation may be all mine.
I resent that he does nothing.
If only he cared he would understand it had to be
And make this easier.

Is he the man he once was?
Am I?
To dance this way is nothing
And simple.

Who was not once dancing and simple?
Stop at that and be of the people.
He could not stop
And was alone.

I know the man who wrote this poem.
I am going home.
He is going home.
Home is a place in a poem.

It is the hour of poem poem.
I will phone it in
On the way home.
Whatever it takes to keep on going.

I ride this into the weeds
With no directions for getting back.
A pastime of getting lost
Rides with me

All the way home,
A habit and a complaint
About blood and soul.
Relax, it takes me a while.

Get sleepy then get wakeful.
Return to the page, squeeze the trigger.
There ought to be a law against this.
The poem is a gun for which there is no permit.

I want to shoot among the trees.
Do I think nature will rescue me?
There is no help in the woods, weeds, road.
I am lost.

All is not lost.
It is still about the poem, the poem
Is on the page being a poem
Alone, with room for doodles in the margins.

It is looking good, even handsome.
Some things should be left alone.
But my fingers are on it.
The poem is.

I write for an audience of one.
It is not me, I will confess.
My secret fan does not protest
I am no hermit.

It is enough for me to be the star,
Which is all that I ask.
The drama is small
But real.

Relax, she is waiting for the poem.
She will not talk to me.
It is a minor thing.
I have no muse.

It is not an excuse
For which I have no use.
She pays attention.
That is all.

Attention must be paid.
I am off in the blue with a shoe shine and a smile.
Poems are my lost children.
They retain their rage on the page.

Anger at the Daddy, an old story
And a good one, stands the test of time.
The poem wants disruption,
Perhaps destruction.

Though I spin and jive,
She is still there, listening intently.
She hears a song
And says yes.

The poem is a relentless nag.
It will not leave me alone.
I feed it with a spoon.
I wipe its ass.

It claims to want freedom,
To stand on its own.
That is what I always thought,
But it is a lie —it is in no rush.

It is my flesh and blood.
It is a child with a temper
Of whom I am proud.
My love is unconditional.

Still, my obligation is to get it to stand up.
So we converse.
It is not always pretty.
I say the wrong thing.

Its legs grow stronger.
It mumbles more.
It says no to me.
It has become a teenager.

I am ready for it to go away to school.
It wants to go to away
But has not figured out how.
It is still young and afraid.

We are across the table and on the same side.
My checkbook is at stake.
Separation puts my heart is on the line.
An old story is real.

Not in the moment, not yesterday, not tomorrow.
To be or not to be.
There is time for that.
Perhaps it is the hour.

That is what this poem pretends.
It is very conventional.
It is something I stand by
Through thick and thin.

Lazy song, will not take up the time.
How do I get back?
I have fond memories of skiing
With grace and speed that sustain me

As I find my way down the hill.
A long drop is comforting.
There is time for this,
A memorial.

It seems to be all over the place,
But it is focused on where it is going
Through the woods to the moment
Of a simple gesture.

It wanders through thickets
To give you its hand.
Cold and then warm.
Each finger is delicate.

Another story ends
Not with a bang, not with a whimper,
Hand in hand.
It is always said.

I cannot get out of the way
Of what I do not remember.
A labor of love with no recall
To complete this.

The lie that this will sing
Is only to myself and mostly harmless.
You hear a recording with a prominent scratch.
Scratch is what I have.

I give what I have.
Warm sounds interrupted annoyingly.
An alarm has gone off in the neighborhood.
Hearts skip a beat.

It is false. This is true.
Hearts skip a beat
While I try to remember
What might have been true.

There is an emotional toll
To these heart beats missed.
The song is unsure
Feeling its way along the wall.

Do not remember what I have forgotten.
See only labor in the vineyard
By a hired hand
Working to some music in the air.

Celebrate this rescued loss
Hearing the tune
In the ear
Of the fool.

This is a found poem.
I found it in my head.
I never would have thought
To look there.

Why should I?
I want to find something self-evident.
Pawing around in the gray matter,
It seems unexpected.

Too much work usually
Goes into the mirror.
Anyway, what is found is found
By this blind one.

Searching takes itself into the poem.
My hands are idle.
They leave me alone
At home with a poem.

I do no work for this.
Still, I am tired.
There is effort looking for gold
Even in your pocket.

I find this here before me.
Nothing is said – it is in your head.
I look in the wrong places
And repeat myself.

That is the way it works.
There is only one song now,
A song of songs disjointed and
Purely bred.

It is laughing as I sit in the dark.
A work of translation from a dead language,
I have no dictionary.
The poem does not care.

I labor away, lost and earnest.
My claim is that I am not at fault
As I try to decipher this.
I will give you cognates for its soul.

It has no regrets,
A function of its manners.
It smiles coolly,
"Sociopath."

I want to be done with it.
I think it is time,
But it has its own rhythms
That I honor.

What in me gives in to this?
I am no fool.
Still, I stay in my chair,
A devoted one.

I complain but there is satisfaction in the effort.
As I discover what it keeps from me
I find small pleasure
In its troubled heart.

Tolerate laughter, ill manners, indifference,
Words with no meaning
All for a little song
Of dubious heritage.

It is shouting at me.
"You are writing a clunker."
Now, waist deep
I plow ahead.

It knows I will not turn back.
It thinks I am a fool.
The poem is usually right.
I do not give a damn.

I have got it where I want it, I think.
I imagine I am on top of it.
It wants light verse
To be perverse.

Big feet, no easy touch,
Heavy forearms,
A loud belch.
It wants to be a greeting card.

This cannot be.
The poem is on its own.
I will see where it wanders.
Will it get this out of its system?

It is worse than I thought.
I was warned.
I did not care—
Just something for me to tame.

Not so simple now.
It writes a poem about a sad girl at home
Alone with a flower that blooms for an hour.
She has blonde hair and I am sorry.

For I do not want to take this with me.
For it is following me.
For it is in drag-along luggage.
For what I want does not matter.

For thee I sing.
For this is not about a cat.
For this is an old story.
For I try to make it new.

For that is a wasted effort.
For the effort must be made.
For this is the product of a little madness.
For it will be indulged.

For no one minds.
For a song should have a refrain.
For wordplay has a heart.
For I am dodging nothing.

For now the target is on my back.
For I must get out in front.
For my desires mean little.
For the pleasure of success may be mine.

For here are the gifts.
For counting the ways is my obligation.
For there might be a God.
For there might be three or four.

For I might be a heretic of conscience.
For I hold on to the obscure.
For I abandon the obvious.
For this would be better about a cat.

Oh shit.
The poem will not right itself.
It remains out of balance.
It is a refusenik.

It wants to leave Russia.
I cannot read the fat novel the poem is in.
I am confused by all the names.
Something is happening in a train station.

Drama accompanies its every word.
That is what happens when you write about love.
How many poems can you write about love?  154.
I am being lazy but it does not matter.

I should not be doing this work.
It can remain off kilter, a tribute to love
In a poem about a poem.
Things can go wrong.

I am out of here.
Abandon all hope ye who enters.
We are in the 20th century stuck
Because we are in century 21.

Modern and post,
There is some irony.
I watch David Letterman.
Hope has not died.

Hope is taking a nap.
It is also falling in love.
All of the above
Is the box I check.

First obsession then art.
An illusion of control.
All is habit.
There is no art in art.

I do this by giving up.
Surrender all hope ye who enters.
I cover my now naked body.
There is great shame.

I am translating from the mother tongue.
A humble chore by a humble servant
Now preening before a mirror.
I will get the words just right.

It hardly matters what I do.
My responsibility is to follow words home.
They get there safely.
I have done my duty.

Vanity, vanity.
I take it with me before the last line.
There is no surprise in this.
There are no fingerprints.

It is graffiti
Plain and simple.
I am a slob spilling this before you
Like creation is a secret.

Show your gratitude.
You get another song.
Hold it against me.
Please.

I am writing this without me.
I do not know what the words are.
The words trip over themselves.
I try to unpile them.

Because I want to.
This is here.
I prefer it not be me.
I would have no hand in this.

It could be free.
I could be free.
Everything could be free.
Instead there is obligation and gesture.

I think kindly upon this
And open my hands to let the bird fly.
See the white dove.
It is a symbol of.

So what.
Be clearheaded about this.
Because I want to
Make the gesture of offering.

This is about itself.
I am about this.
It is out of control.
The obligation does not cease.

Cool it down.
Calm it down.
It is coming down now.
It looks for a prize.

An elegy for what never was
Is the usual situation.
The habit of longing writes these words.
I want to leave this house.

Taking a walk down the street.
Wanting desire interrupted.
It is the trees and the flowers
That make this moment.

Hope, hope, hope,
I want to take this walk without leaving.
I will stay home and make something of this.
The longing is constant.

I want to know why I am doing this.
The desire to know is not greater than the act.
I am satisfied blind.
Ambition is ignorant.

I am comfortable waiting for it to bubble up
From my feet.  It may be heartless but
It will do.
Follow it all the way out.

Bring it all the way home.
I stop to eat a sandwich, peel an orange.
This comes from nothing driving away
And wanting to rest.

All my heart is out going away.
This is the best I can hope.
What slips from mind
Is never here.

The air is quiet.
The room is dark.
I want you.
I have you.

It is always a surprise
When the poem turns from itself.
I am writing this.
I am with you.

It is simple to be two places at once.
I have my hands all over.
The unexpected is always present.
You are everything.

I turn from the poem.
The poem follows me into you
Lying on the bed like a cat.
We are in the kitchen eating soup.

This is erotic literature in which no one touches.
It is touching.
The steam from the soup.
I turn up the light.

It is cold and it is sunny.
I need more light.
You are content with the light from the window.
We have never agreed.

It does not matter.
A line between us is traced in steam.
The poem is quiet.
We pass through.

This crusade is becoming a bore.
I want to do comedy.
I am standing up.
A standup guy.

The stage beckons.
I think I can.
One line at a time
Is all I know.

Limited knowledge follows me onto the boards.
I try a line.
It was supposed to be an easy laugh.
I am more afraid.

I return to the page
Burdened with a theme.
The paper is a mirror revealing
Nose and mouth and words.

Nothing is golden.
I am recording this,
A live performance
In a small space.

Sitting down for this
I cannot take a bow.
It is an odd campaign
To see and be seen.

On paper it looks sorry.
There is no joke.
Only ambition and confused desire
Propel the hand.

It is a poor imitation.
I creep in, always here.
Trying to be the other guy,
Who I am not.

Driven by jealousy
I try to be not me.
I fail and live by my own words.
It is a contest lost.

No $500 prize and publication in.
Alone with my thoughts.
Residual anger.
I care.

I look into a book.
I just want to borrow a little bit.
I will return it sometime soon,
With interest.

Imitation is the sincerest form of flattery.
Take it where you can get it, please.
My interest is passing.
You will always be you.

I said it will not be good.
Low fidelity will protect you.
No one will know.
This is how it has always worked.

So much anxiety.
I write what I cannot help.
You are stuck with me
For a brief moment.

Dirty with words I am unclean.
I wash my hands.
I hope for the best.
It is not my usual custom.

My habit is to be without hope.
But on this snowy day I am sunny.
An escape does come.
My hands smell fresh.

The dirt of the words is with me.
I have skipped a day
And the body needs a scrubbing.
This only seems simple.

I present with clean hands.
Pink and fleshy,
They reveal nothing that I have hidden.
Still, this is hard.

It is hard to roll with it.
It is hard
To find the words in the soil,
The litter, the garbage.

My desire, my errand is everything.
I present with clean hands
This fine little song, now ready for consumption.
Consumption is not the disease of the age.

Dirt is the remaining plague.
It must be wiped out.
Clean hands are insufficient.
Oh, for a vaccination.

The page is a wall on which nothing sticks.
I have to nail every word down.
It always says the same thing –
Bristol was here.

The paper is hard.
The nails bend under the hammer.
It looks like a tagged subway car.
Can you read this?

It has some color.
It is a virtuoso performance.
The strings get tugged.
I like mixed media.

At least I try.
Can this be read any other way?
Find the loss and the hope in this.
Persistence.

I am leaving here what I have found.
So be it.
The words are not straight.
I use no level – just a hammer.

The tools are as limited as the words.
The vocabulary of the poem is stunted.
It cries out for new terms, another bargain
That leaves me out.

This will lie on the page, alone.
I have run away.
I wore gloves.
There are no prints.

Between plodding and mania
There is heart.
I have heart.
I am stuck.

It is no place to be in the morning.
The paper has its hand out to me.
So inviting.
I am a believer.

A cautions move is required.
The language of what does not flow
Is with me.
My hand rests on the table.

I plod and wish for mania.
A coward's way out.
Hard work looks easy.
I am fooled by myself.

It is not that I am lazy.
It is that I want to loaf in grace.
Wear a hat, grow a beard.
Walt never let you see the head banging.

I know it is true.
There is heart in this gesture.
I know it is true.
I lift my hand and hit the keys.

Something will be there.
I have no headache.
Something gets easier—
Accepting anything.

I am here without flowers.
I always neglect the flowers.
I am here, always.
No flowers are my loss.

It is an anniversary and I am forgetful.
It would be graceful to have flowers.
A dozen roses would be right
In my hand about now.

The poet should think of this.
But that is a myth.
I am clueless
As to gestures of the heart.

Yes, I give a kiss.
Of course, I remember the day.
I never miss a year.
But I tend to my own thoughts.

This cannot be written as a poem.
It will not be.
I have no motorcycle, no opera shoes.
A lean moment for imagination.

This is only the text of what might have been.
A description of the moment three days later
Emerges in prose.
I sling it around

Into seven stanzas.
I think I can, I think I can.
I give it up
In surrender.

Little control of what gets onto the page.
Mostly a function of rage.
Untempered by age.
There is a rattle in this cage.

Though I indulge a habit
I am not a Babbitt.
I am not from the Midwest.
It does not matter.

I repeat songs but not lyrics.
It is the nature of the game.
False humility touches everything.
I touch this.

There is no image or metaphor.
It tries to be a poem.
It partakes of said qualities.
Now it is a contract

For your pleasure.
I am trapped in a loop of fine words
And mixed intention
And lost rhythms.

Honesty is the best policy.
Honesty will never do.
A pugnacious pose would add some spice.
My fist is not in it.

I am no prizefighter.
This is no prize.
It tries for a rise.
Then it turns subtle.

Without an image to live up to.
Without an image to live down.
No graven images.
I follow the commandments.

I take a walk.
Step lightly, but do not know where
On a street I know – I live here.
I try to be lost.

In the moment. On the spot. At the desk.
It is no place to be.
I am grateful there is plenty of time
To work this out, up and down.

Nowhere to go, I am out and about.
Unsuccessful at getting lost.
I recognize the lights in the windows
Close to where I started.

An old tune accompanies me.
Honor thy father and thy mother.
Do not steal, etc.
I cannot get it out of my head.

Now, I cannot dance.
I walk, easy steps.
This is governed by laws I subscribe to.
I am a Jew.

It would be nice if this worked out.
If things were settled the way they are.
I hold an image in my hand.
It is not graven.

The grand finale has a smile and a tear.
The credits roll in a dark room.
Read the names that pass too quickly.
Hold onto the moment.

Sentiment cluttered with popcorn
Is what I have been waiting for.
How many love poems can you read?
I will finish this and more.

Now I am concentrating on the end.
It has come to me before I am ready.
The mail has landed on the floor.
My mind has wandered

From the film that warmed me.
There is nothing wrong with this.
I want to tend to something else.
It is the ending I do not want now.

Smile and tear is nice.
Something always to be ready for.
But not constantly desired.
Constant desire for food and love.

Welcome an unexpected change of pace.
I thought it would be an easy out.
Appetite and lust turn on me.
Everything is out of place.

I thought I knew the ending
Would have luster.
Cluttered sentiment.
I thought I knew the ending.

Buried alive is my current state.
Cannot move my fingers, cannot read the gauges.
It may be something that I ate.
It is a story for the ages.

I swing for the bleachers
And abuse a sports metaphor.
I have no business with this.
What I watch on TV does not matter.

It is a story from the ages.
It is not mine.
Still, I repeat it.
All the world is on stages and in cages.

I am in a petting zoo.
Children can touch me.
I wait and do not know what to do.
My hair is longer than I remembered.

The dictionary is out of alphabetical order.
The words I want to know are lost forever.
Nothing is verified.
They have placed me in a zoo to preserve the species.

Protected and fed on schedule
I grind out words I cannot define.
I cannot know what I mean.
I rely on habit.

It is almost over.
The children are leaving for the day.
I have been touched.
It is that easy and that hard.

I read a poem and then another.
Nothing registers.
Left to my own devices, I want to marry this.
I propose a nice wedding,

A romantic honeymoon.
It is what I want, desperately.
We are happy with my devices.
Here and now.

Left to my own devices, I conceive of you.
We are joined at the hip.
Something old, something new, something borrowed, something blue
Is how it is.

There is hope in this habit of getting lost.
I pretend it is a marriage because it is a marriage
Of hope and habit
To which I bring love and loss.

All that I have is here.
This was never my intention.
I just wanted a beginning.
Now, I share a household.

It is a victory of sorts.
It got started and all is arrayed before me.
I will need to have a yard sale
To see what remains.

One poem and then another, I look again.
There is nothing but what I make.
You are here.
I am here.

There is snow on the ground.
I want to muscle through this.
It is not a nature poem.
Muscle beach. Muscle car. I hope.

I will lay my cards on the table.
I like the light off the snow.
The natural world creeps in.
A battle royale.

There is snow on the ground without blood.
My muscles are working too hard.
I have no control.
I am ashamed.

So much conflict.
I put my hand to this
With a soft touch.
The snow is quieter than me.

I have my wish.
Snow does not melt in my glove.
I have come out for the light.
I am alone in this.

There is no fight or flight.
What started in difficulty ends at peace.
Simple beyond my dreams,
I surrender to the snow and the leaf.

The force on my hand is me.
Not daring, it retreats.
No muscle.
A plot of land with snow.

I believe in the system.
I get up.  I sit down.
I turn on the machine.
The system believes in me.

It is the morning.
It is every morning.
I am a subscriber.
My subscription ends next year.

This will end happily.
It is the product of habit.
I have all the time in the world
To put my feet up.

To put my feet up
Is to trust time.
I do not believe I have an hour or a day.
Now or never.  Plunge ahead.

But I am sitting in repose.
To take what is here.
Not to leave it to chance.
I have no trust.

I try my luck, pressing the keys.
There are words for this.
The process is overwhelming.
I am out of bed.

There are words from this
Spilled on the page.
I surrender to the disorder.
A believer.

Up the air I leave you.
THE END is only the beginning.
I finished this before I started.
It is that time of day.

If only my timing was good
I would be at some other point,
Not confused about the beginning or ending
Of this circle.

A clock with no numbers.
Time is running out.
I do not know when,
Morning or afternoon.

I go in a circle,
Not knowing where I am.
Knowing only that I am here.
Utterances.

Ill-timed, I lay it out.
I spill the beans.
But I am confused
About beginning of the end

Or the end of the beginning.
A simple desire to know where you are.
These are difficulties, always present.
It makes me shy away.

From desire to desire
I proceed, unsure of my footing.
I prefer the beginning of the end.
Something is ahead of me.

David Bristol attended New York University and the George Washington University Law School. He practiced law for 37 years. His poems have been published in numerous magazines and anthologies. He is the author of three earlier collections of poetry.

www.ingramcontent.com/pod-product-compliance
Lightning Source LLC
Chambersburg PA
CBHW032100150426
43194CB00006B/595